MONASTIC WISDOM SERIES: NUMBER ELEVEN

André Louf, ocso

The Way of Humility

D0871057

MONASTIC WISDOM SERIES

Patrick Hart, OCSO, General Editor

Advisory Board

Michael Casey, OCSO   Terrence Kardong, OSB
Lawrence S. Cunningham   Kathleen Norris
Bonnie Thurston   Miriam Pollard, OCSO

MONASTIC WISDOM SERIES: NUMBER ELEVEN

The Way of Humility

by

André Louf, ocso

Translated and introduced by

Lawrence S. Cunningham

CISTERCIAN PUBLICATIONS
Kalamazoo, Michigan

Originally published as *L'umiltà* by Edizioni Qiqajon,
Monasterio de Bose, Magnano (Italy).

Cistercian Publications
Editorial Offices
The Institute of Cistercian Studies
Western Michigan University
Kalamazoo, Michigan 49008-5415
cistpub@wmich.edu

*The work of Cistercian Publications is made possible in part by support from
Western Michigan University to The Institute of Cistercian Studies.*

Library of Congress Cataloging-in-Publication Data

Louf, André.
    [L'umiltà. English]
    The way of humility / by André Louf ; translated with an
introduction by Lawrence S. Cunningham.
        p. cm. — (Monastic wisdom series ; no. 11)
    Originally published : L'umiltà. Edizioni Qiqajon, Monasterio
de Bose, Magnano (Italy).
    Includes bibliographical references and index.
    ISBN-13: 978-0-87907-011-3
    ISBN-10: 0-87907-011-0
        1. Humility—Religious aspects—Catholic Church.   2. Spiritual
life—Catholic Church.   3. Desert Fathers.   I. Title.   II. Series.
    BV4647.H8L6813 2007
    241'.4—dc22   2007007731

Printed in the United States of America

TABLE OF CONTENTS

FOREWORD

André Louf was born in the Belgian university city of Louvain in 1929. At the age of twenty-two he entered the Cistercian abbey of Mont-des-Cats in northern France where he was ordained to the priesthood in 1955. Dom Louf studied both at the Gregorian University in Rome and the Biblical Institute. When he returned to his abbey he edited the review *Collectanea Cisterciensia* but in 1963, at the extraordinarily young age of 33, he was elected abbot of his monastery, an office he held until his retirement in 1997. Today, he lives in solitude near a monastery in Provence.

The bare bones of the biography described above gives very little indication of the esteem in which he is held in Europe. In 1968 he, along with Thomas Merton and the Procurator of the Carthusian Order, was asked by the late Pope Paul VI to compose the "Letter from Contemplatives" which was subsequently to appear in English in Thomas Merton's posthumous volume *The Monastic Journey*. The University of Louvain granted him an honorary doctorate in 1994 as a way to pay tribute both to his scholarly and spiritual accomplishments. Some of his many works have been translated into English (see the bibliography) but they give scant witness to his reputation on the other side of the Atlantic. One indicator of that reputation is that in 2004 Pope John Paul II asked him to write the meditations for the Way of the Cross held at the Colosseum in Rome for the annual Good Friday services held there each year.

One of the many services that he has extended to the worldwide monastic family was to give his encouragement and to share his wisdom with the new monastic community of Bose in Northern Italy, a mixed community of some seventy men and women, where the conferences which make up this little book were first given. The text of those conferences was first published by that monastery's publishing house *Qiqajon* (the name comes from the Hebrew word for the ivy plant that shaded the prophet Jonah) and later in France by *Editions Parole et Silence* (2002) under the title *Humilité* from which this present translation is based.

The theme of humility in Christian spirituality is a vast one. The entry under that word in the authoritative *Dictionnaire de Spiritualité* runs to many double-columned pages. Humility is a core idea in the monastic tradition as every person familiar with the *Rule of Benedict* (and its gloss by Saint Bernard of Clairvaux) knows only too well. "Love and humility make a holy team," Saint John Climacus writes in step twenty-five of *The Ladder of Monks*, "The one exalts and the other supports those who have been exalted and never falls."

This little book, it is scarcely more than a longish pamphlet, would seem incapable of saying something new about the topic which is found everywhere in the monastic literature but, in fact, Dom Louf has something quite important to say and that "something important" has to do with how he reorders our understanding of humility as a "virtue."

When one consults the exhaustive Kittel's *Theological Dictionary of the New Testament* for the meaning of the Greek word *tapeinos* and its cognates it is abundantly clear that in the Greek and Hellenistic world *tapeinos* as well as those cognates, is a term almost universally used in a pejorative sense. Humility resonates with the state of being lowly, servile, mean, insignificant, and so on. The humble person is, by turns, a servile subject or, as one in reaction to that condition, a flatterer. In either case, it is not a term of endearment.

The pejorative understanding of humility found in the classical sources does not carry over into the Bible. Humility becomes a term used variously in a positive manner in the Hebrew scriptures either as a concept used to describe one's relationship to the God of the Covenant or as a word to describe the humble ones who receive the covenant and live by it.

In the New Testament, by contrast to the classical tradition, *tapeinos* and its cognates occur thirty-four times with some frequency both in Matthew and Luke (but not in John) and the letters of Paul. Every person who is even casually informed by the New Testament knows that humility is a term that has a positive ring to it whether describing a necessary characteristic of the true disciple of Jesus or, in the magnificent hymn which Paul gives us in the second chapter of Philippians, a signal action of Jesus Christ who humbled himself unto death, even death on a cross. Both in the preeminent example of Jesus and, by extension, the disciples of Jesus in general and Mary significantly in her *Magnificat*, the essential dynamic is from humiliation to exaltation. Summing up the history of the word, the *Theological Dictionary of the New Testament* states: "The Greek view of humility exalts freedom and despises subjection. Hence it qualifies *tapeinos* negatively. The Bible sets humility under God and thus extolls obedient service. Hence it gives the *tapeinos* group a positive sense" [*TDNT*: sub voce].

Dom Louf, understanding this distinction well, points out that when the later Christian intellectual tradition attempted to analyze humility under the rubric of virtue understood in the Greek sense of *arete* (a word scarcely and ambiguously used in the New Testament as he notes) it had a difficult time to give it the priority demanded by the New Testament evidence. Hence, Louf's strategy is, in these pages, to abandon the largely Aristotelean category of virtue (*arete*) and recover in a stunning example of *ressourcement* the earlier, mainly monastic, sense of humility as it is reflected in the monastic and ascetic literature of both East and West. That sense, of course, has its roots in the New Testament *anawim*—those poor ones who hear the Gospel but its root goes deeper in the piety of the Hebrew people.

By holding together two words that derive from the same root he can analyze both humiliation and humility in a rigorous fashion. What is more fascinating is that he does this, as he remarks in passing, against the discordant voice(s) of both the tradition of the masters of suspicion springing from the well springs of both Nietzsche and Freud as well as the striving voices of neoliberal political and economic thought which not only do not value humility but manifest themselves in almost heroic opposition. Louf does not make the point expressly but what those two strains of modern and postmodern thought value is a dim view of humility almost identical to that of ancient Greek thought. The conclusion, of course, is that the Christian view of humility, like the larger phenomenon of monasticism itself is, and correctly so, counter-cultural. What Louf sketches out in a few pages makes one yearn for somebody to take up his analysis and pursue it further. In other words, what these pages reflect is not a finished work but an opening into a theme which deserves greater reflection. By making this work accessible to an English reading public, may it challenge someone to take up Louf's theme and pursue it further for it is eminently worthy of further exploration.

* * * * * * * * * *

A word about this translation. The footnotes in part one are those which Dom Louf himself supplied. He uses such notes sparingly. Many, but not all, the readings from the texts in part two were culled by the original author from his own vast reading. Some of these readings do not exist in easily accessible English translations and a few are not translated into English at all, so I simply translated them directly from the French. To the texts Louf appended to his essay I have added some fundamental texts from the New Testament with the intention of enlarging Louf's analysis in the text of his essay.

A portion of part one of this little book was put into a first draft in English by my doctoral student, Krista Duttenhover but I went over the whole so any mistakes are mine and not hers. I have added a select bibliography for further reading at the end of the book for those who are interested in pursuing some of the themes and sources treated by Louf in this little book. I did not add any works on the subject of humility itself since that would overly burden the bibliography due to the huge number of essays and books written on that theme in the literature.

As I was finishing this translation I discovered that part one of this book had been translated into English and published as a pamphlet by the Catholic Truth Society in England without Louf's notes and omitting the supporting texts. Through the kindness of my colleague Professor Paul Bradshaw I obtained a copy of that pamphlet and compared it to my own efforts.

Finally, let me express my thanks to the Monastic Wisdom Series of Cistercian Publications for allowing me the opportunity of spending some months in the company of Dom André Louf's profound thinking. I would like to thank Professor Rozanne Elder and Brother Patrick Hart for their friendship and support. I am also always grateful to my colleagues in the Department of

Theology at the University of Notre Dame for making this such a congenial place to work.

This manuscript was finished on the Feast of the Sorrows of the Blessed Virgin Mary (September 15, 2006)—a wonderful day to write about humility.

I would like to dedicate this little effort to Brother Patrick Hart, ocso, monk of Gethsemani, who, over the decades, has been a friend and an inspiration to me and my work.

Lawrence S. Cunningham
John A. O'Brien Professor of Theology
The University of Notre Dame

PART I

INTRODUCTION

One day, the *Apothegmata* tells us, Saint Anthony stepped out of his hermitage where he saw all the snares of the devil spread out like a net over the world. He let out a great groan of terror and cried out: "My God! How can anyone be saved?" A voice responded from heaven: "Humility."[1] Consider that saying in the light of another one from the same Anthony: "Without temptations, no person can be saved."[2] The conclusion is quite clear: As much as temptations are inevitable in the Christian life, they also clearly demand the practice of humility.

"Humility in the monastic life" is the theme that has been proposed for me; proposed but with a sweet and amicable pressure that I have been unable to resist. Quickly, however, there arises a bit of a quandary. By what right do I have to speak about humility? Am I to consider myself as an expert on this topic? Or: do I set myself up as an example? Who would dare make such a claim since, at the same time, it would be clear proof that one totally lacked humility? "To assert that one is not proud," says Saint John Climacus, "is one of the clearest proofs that one is proud."[3] To believe oneself to be humble is still worse. It leaves one open to ridicule.

Let me add a second trap: the mention of the monastic life as the place for inquiry. Is humility to be the realm of monks? Are they the ones who are more advanced in humility than other Christians? I do not think so! Far from it! Indeed, I would be bold enough to say: quite the contrary. The very status which is theirs, that of the monastic life, exposes them, more than to others, to think better of themselves. In those discriminating pages

1. Saying of Anthony: 5.
2. Saying of Anthony: 7.
3. *The Ladder of Divine Ascent*—Step 23.

where the shrewdness of psychological analysis has never been surpassed, Saint John Cassian has described, even for the most advanced ascetics, how the final evil ruse of the devil has turned to his profit the vainglory the most beautiful exploits of asceticism. The spirit of vainglory ensnares a monk by a subtle trap (an image which he uses) to safeguard one's self love with a false humility which becomes a last refuge. Cassian then illustrates his analysis with some rapid sketches: "If he (the devil) cannot drag a person down by honor, he overthrows him by humility. If he cannot make him proud by the grace of knowledge and eloquence, he pulls him down by the weight of silence. If a monk fasts openly, he is attacked by the pride of vanity. . . In order to avoid vainglory he avoids making prayers in the sight of his brethren and yet because he offers them in secret and no one is conscious of it, he does not escape the pride of vanity." In short, it is the very path of monastic living where there are hidden the snares which can make one fall.[4] Thus one can understand the extreme difficulty in making a judicious discernment between true and false humility.

Nor is humility an easy topic to speak of, particularly, today, for other reasons. All of the great "masters of suspicion" have called the issue into question. In the eyes of Nietzsche, humility is the great lie of the weak that cunningly transforms cowardice into apparent virtue. For Freud it is a form of the masochistic guilt complex. For Adler, it runs close to a feeling of inferiority. Their analyses have left their mark on our modern culture. How can we reconcile humility with that famous "assertiveness," so extolled by those psychologists from across the Atlantic, and for some reason also? How honor the "last place" according to the Gospel in a society so singularly impressed by the success of the "Young Turks"[5] or in the political realm by the "golden boys" in economics?

An Ambiguous Situation

I would further like to call your attention to another issue, perhaps less recognized, it seems to me, but for all that, more

4. *The Institutes* XI.4.
5. Literally: The "Young Wolves" (trans).

problematic, which is responsible for our difficulties when we attempt to speak clearly today about Christian humility. This problematic has deep roots in the history of spirituality and lingers today in an unrecognized fashion in many souls. It expresses itself in a certain ambiguity which has become attached to the notion of humility. On one hand, from scripture and the tradition, spiritual authors accord humility an eminent place in experience but, on the other hand, it is conceptualized in a schema which places it as one of the "Christian virtues" which creates the difficulty of giving it the priority corresponding to the eminence which all the world sees in a light quite different from that of the saying of Anthony cited above.

A more precise analysis for the reasons of this problematic is beyond the range of this conference but a little can be said here. When seen in the light of the gospel and the experience of the great spiritual writers, it seems that the very ambiguity of the notion of "virtue" might be the problem. The usual understanding of the word "virtue" (*arete*) is found among the words of Jesus or in the gospels. The two letters of Peter use the word three times but in two places it refers to God and is a synonym for the "glory of God."[6] The third citation appears in a pair of qualities demanded of the believer, as an intensive of "faith" and "knowledge."[7]

Saint Paul uses the word one time, one would say, in passing, in Philippians 4:8 where virtue (*arete*) is found among a list of other Christian qualities and serves as a synonym for "good reputation."[8] Paul is not thinking at all of the concept of virtue as it was employed by Greek philosophers. The Syriac version of the passage, perhaps reflecting an even more ancient Aramaic translation, gets closer to the best reading: it translates: "works of glory and praise" about the works, which, in the context of the epistle, Paul hopes that their works reflected in the manner of their life become known and esteemed by their contemporaries.

The problem of humility understood as a virtue shows up in the patristic literature remaining right down to the middle

6. I Peter 2:9; II Peter 1:3.
7. II Peter 1:5; the NRSV translates it as "goodness."
8. NRSV: "commendable."

ages. On the one hand, there is unanimity in which everyone gives humility not only pride of place but judges it absolutely fundamental for the spiritual path. In Augustine, for example, it sums up the whole of Christian ascesis: *Humilitas pene una disciplina christiana est.*[9] For Cassian it is "the mother and mistress of all the virtues" and he adds an important qualification to situate it in relation to pagan virtues: "it is the precise and magnificent gift of the Savior."[10] One could multiply the citations.

On the other hand, the same patristic tradition found a certain problem in expressing this absolute primacy within the categories of moral philosophy which it had been forced to borrow in order to define a Christian ethic. We find ourselves here in the presence of a typical case of the inculturation of the faith in a milieu which is not preeminently adapted to it. It is a case, moreover, which quite instructive. A certain degree of inculturation is absolutely necessary, indeed, unavoidable, for it happens in any event despite us and, perhaps, in spite of us. Inculturation, however, always carries a risk. Indeed, faith itself experiences itself as threatened by more or less being tempted away from itself or even deformed in one fashion or another according to the particular characteristics in which it comes to exist. Furthermore, with respect to humility, we would do well to ask ourselves whether, in ths process of inculturation, it did not fall victim to certain noxious corruptions.

This risk clearly grows when one theorizes about humility without having any authentic experience of it. As Pseudo-Macarius noted: Christianity runs the risk of getting carried away bit by bit beyond its limits so that it will end up having the same significance as atheism. A formidable risk, indeed! For such realities, he adds "are accomplished mysteriously in the heart by the work of the Holy Spirit and it is for that reason alone that one can speak of them."[11]

Did there exist a "pagan humility?" The most acute sages of the great patristic epoch could not avoid that question since most of them were anxious to discover among the thinkers of antiquity

9. Sermon 351.3.4.
10. *Conferences* 15.7.
11. *Discourse* 80.

some intimations of the realities of the Christian faith already embedded in their thought as an effect of grace. The subject was debated with the Greek Fathers sympathetic to their cultural brethren. Clement of Alexandria, for example, thought that he detected humility in a text from Plato.[12] Origen, in his gloss on the *Magnificat* and the humility of the Virgin explained that the ancient philosophers recognized this virtue under the name of *metriotes*—(measure)[13] which was to become in Latin "moderation" *(mediocritas)* and, as a consequence, he started a perilous path, sown with traps, but onto which Saint Thomas (with practically all the spiritual writers after him) ventured gladly.

Saint Augustine seems to have been the first to insist forcefully on the exclusive Christian character of humility while denying that the pagan authors, whether Epicurean, Stoic, or Platonist, possessed the concept. Even the greatest of the pagans, Saint Augustine said, disregarded humility because, he claimed, "humility comes from elsewhere, from the One who, being the Most High, wished to empty Himself for us."[14] What the bishop of Hippo expressed there as a spiritual thinker basically reaffirms what so many spiritual men and women, in accord with the saying of Saint Antony cited above, already lived out and expressed in their own fashion.

Nonetheless, the idea that there was a kind of humility acceptable in the eyes of the ancient philosophers has had a long and tenacious existence. In fact, it can be asked whether such a notion survives in a more or less aggressive fashion in the consciousness of contemporary Christian culture. It is possible that Saint Thomas Aquinas might be held culpable for this holdover. As noted above, the Angelic Doctor at first, a bit put out that humility was not on Aristotle's list of virtues, took as his own Origen's assertion that identified humility with the Platonic concept of *metriotes*; this would make humility into a species of moderation, measure, temperance. A risky move. Saint Thomas, in fact, categorizes Christian humility as a by-product (if one dares use the word) of the virtue of temperance. He explains his judgment:

12. *Stromata* II.22.
13. *Homilies on Luke* 8:4-5.
14. *Ennarationes in Ps* 2 31:18.

humility is a virtue of suppression for its task is to rein in the appetite and desire which, without the virtue of humility, would tend to employ all its energies to desire that which is *praeter rationem*—against right reason. Thus, Aristotle is called to the rescue along with Cicero whom Thomas follows in describing humility as falling under the rubric of modesty.[15]

Saint Thomas's task was a delicate one. He was attempting to safeguard the heart of the catalogue of philosophical virtues as a precise equilibrium between a virtue and its opposite by setting up a virtuous *mediocritas: In Medio stat virtus*—virtue stands in the medium. But from Aristotle's perspective the opposite of moderation is magnanimity which cannot be eroded by too much self depreciation. Saint Thomas, attentive to this issue, gave himself over to an almost charming set of dialectical contortions in order to safeguard humility (which the Greeks almost wholly disregarded) and a kind of magnanimity which was at least as secular or political as it was Christian in character.

Let us not cast stones at Saint Thomas who possessed the great merit of engaging, to a vast degree with success, the inculturation of the Gospel with the thought of Aristotle. Still, we might inquire whether, in such a system, humility might find itself a bit constricted or even demoted from the central role it plays in Christian experience.

In a number of places which will not be discussed here, Saint Thomas, perhaps not pleased with his explanation, tried to reconfigure the equilibrium with a larger emphasis on humility. The Aristotelian Christians of the later middle ages failed to do as much themselves. Siger of Brabant, an Aristotelian of the strict observance, pushed to the limit ancient thought. For him, "magnanimity is a more perfect virtue than humility" with humility being the virtue of the "less perfect ones"—the mediocre ones— whereas magnanimity is the privilege of the strong.[16] Here we are in view of Nietzschean concepts! Where do we find ourselves if we take that road? Moreover, we might raise the following objection: "And Jesus on the cross—was he magnanimous or humble?"

15. *Summa* II IIae IV.
16. *Questiones Morales* I.

Indeed, reaction to that position was not long in coming. It came from a theologian in the line of Saint Francis. Francis, by his own admission, saw poverty and humility as two sisters whom he wished his followers to obey. What is more, he chose for those followers the beautiful name of lesser brothers (*fratres minores*). It is Saint Bonaventure who reacted strongly against the Aristotelean position. In his view, it would be perfectly foolish to retrieve the notion of Christian humility from Aristotle's work or to explicate it from the vantage point of human reason. Humility can only be understood in the context of Jesus Christ. And he went on to say that if only our ears would cease to listen to this so-called magnanimity which poses such a threat to humility we would then see that true magnanimity is humility![17]

This rapid overview of some of the conflicts which have plagued the discussion of humility throughout the history of spirituality is sufficient to clarify the paradoxical and precarious situation of humility from an evangelical perspective. If the learned ones of the spiritual life experience some ambiguity about correctly classifying humility in the heart of the list of virtues derived from pagan origins, the same could not be said of those who possessed some experiential knowledge of humility. We have already cited some who have expressed themselves on this subject but we could provide a long list of testimonials who would attest to its exceptional importance. Two final examples must suffice to convince us. A mother of the desert named Theodora—for there were authentic mothers of the desert as well as fathers—underscored the importance of humility without mincing words: "It is neither asceticism nor vigils nor any other work which saves us; only sincere humility."[18] Isaac the Syrian underscores the statement making it even more peremptory: "Without even works, humility obtains pardon . . . but without humility works are of no profit. What salt is to food, humility is to the virtues but without humility all our works are in vain—indeed, all our virtues and our asceticism."[19] Isaac says it well: the salt of virtues. If one recognizes it as a virtue it will still be necessary to see it as

17. *De perfectione Evangelica: Quaestio de Humilitate* ad 1.
18. *Apothegmata: Theodora: 6.*
19. Discourse 57.

a virtue wholly set apart. Saint Basil held on to a term borrowed from philosophy calling humility *panaretos*—the total or complete virtue;[20] a virtue we might call all encompassing because it contains within itself all the others.

Humility: The Experience of a Journey

But if one felt it necessary to make humility a virtue and, more to the point, to make it a standard of measurement for the greater or lesser esteem that it bears on one's self, we run the risk of considerably weakening its significance. So, in the second part of this exploration I would like to present humility from the perspective of the traits embodied in concrete experience which is both connected to particular situations and properly scriptural—an experience that the early monks actually lived out and described as an essential stage of Christian living. We will ask ourselves about that which concretely takes place in that experience while attempting to describe how one conducts onself in such an experience.

It is not a question of the *virtue* of humility but rather the *state* of humility, that is, in the original sense of the Greek word *tapeinosis*—the state of abasement or in Latin: *humilitas/humus*—the condition in which one finds onself flatly on the ground. A state which is absolutely indispensable in order that a virtue (in Greek we could call this *tapeinophrosune*) might be born. Indeed, Saint Bernard has observed: *sine humiliatione, nulla humilitas*—that is, without quite concrete abasement, there can be no humility.

It lies beyond the scope of this investigation to dwell at length on the christological root of this notion of abasement. Saint Paul magnificently casts light upon abasement in his hymn found in his letter to the Philippians with its double movement of elevation of descent and elevation: He was humbled and that is why he was exalted.[21] This is the double dynamic that Jesus must have offered more than once to his disciples since we find this theme described more than once in the Synoptics and elsewhere in the New Testament as well: "Whoever humbles himself will be

20. *De Renuntiatione Saeculi* 9 (see: *Const. Mon 9*).
21. Louf encapsulates Phil 2 here.

exalted."[22] God took it upon himself to direct gently anyone who refuses to move towards such an experience: "And you Capernaum, do you believe that you will be elevated to the heavens? Into hell will you be cast."[23] That hell which, even as Jesus speaks of it, is none other than that place he soon will go, reconciling it to himself in triumph by his death.

With respect to talk about the humility of Jesus, it is not a question of some quality he had in order to demonstrate it for us but rather, to the contrary, a genuine salvific journey, the first stage of which consists in an unavoidable abasement. It is a question of the paschal journey to which, in imitation of Jesus, every Christian is invited. For Jesus, this journey was one of confrontation with the Prince of Evil from the very first temptation in the desert to the culminating point in the garden of Gethsemane and on to the passion of the cross. For the disciples, the journey will be equally marked by temptation—that ineluctable temptation which is the sole path of salvation. That is the deeper meaning of Antony's saying: "Remove all temptations and no one will be saved." To wish to avoid them would be futile; sooner or later it is necessary to march through them. There is no way out neither for the monk in the desert nor the Christian in the world since both the world and the desert are places of temptation. The only difference between the two is that the monk, guided by the Spirit, has chosen, so to speak, to walk towards temptation.

In a brief utterance spoken when he himself, sorrowful unto death, was in the grips of his own decisive temptation Jesus described for his apostles what takes place at the heart of temptation: "The spirit is strong but the flesh is weak. Watch and pray that you might not fail at the hour of temptation."[24] Two opposing forces confront each other here battling for control of the heart of Jesus and that of his disciples: the flesh, infirm and feeble, and the spirit that of a man but also that of God, both ardent, forceful and yet terribly encumbered by the pressures of the flesh. Jesus counsels two things: watchfulness and prayer. For it is at the heart of temptation more than anywhere else that the believer, already

22. Mt 23:12; Lk 14:11; 18:14.
23. Lk 10:15.
24. Mt 26:41.

weakened by complicity with the flesh, experiences the necessity of God's aid: he cries out for help. It is there, at the center of the crisis (we are talking about a genuine crisis here) that a true humility, like a gift from the Spirit, is born. This humility alone allows the believer to pass through temptation with a minimum of risk.

This conflict between flesh and spirit, between sin and grace, between the human and the Spirit of God implies an awareness, at one and the same time, of both the vertiginous weakness of the potential sinners that we are and the gentle and delicate (but finally irresistible) power of grace. Better than most, Saint John Cassian knew how to describe the significant risks in this struggle to the point that it happens so persistently that one runs the risk of a fall. Along with this awareness of weakness another awareness establishes itself holding the first in some equilibrium. It is in the grip of temptation that one perceives the action of grace in himself, in and through the groans wrenched out of him by the very force of the assault which, in turn, nourishes his prayer and makes it constant.

"We must ourselves learn," writes Cassian, "to feel in each action both our weakness and the help of God and to proclaim daily with the saints 'I was hard pressed and was falling but the Lord helped me/My strength and my courage is the Lord/and he has been my savior'" (Ps 117:13-14).[25]

Cassian has just told us that we must understand both our "weakness and the help of God." A recently discovered text of Isaac the Syrian (the original in Syriac is no longer extant) describes with a different vocabulary the very same disjunction of sin and grace. Isaac exhorts the solitary monk to attend carefully to the succession of consolations and temptations in his heart. It is in such a way that he will learn to recognize both his own weakness and the power of grace. "Solitary monks," says Isaac, "who attend to their hearts in all their ascetic struggles see this force spiritually . . . they sense when grace departs and also when it approaches. They are aware of the change which is produced in them both by the inexpressible force which they suddenly feel in their hearts and by their own weakness. Very often, this force

25. *Institutes* XII: 17.1.

alters the body at the same time as the spirit. What insight has come to one who has experienced this! My brothers, we must agree to reflect carefully about this awareness. On account of this continual reflection upon what takes place at the time of temptation, the one who educates himself in this fashion acquires a great and profound humility as well as an unshakeable faith in God."[26]

What is the role of a man in this combat which is at the heart of temptation? It is simply stated according to Cassian: *ut quotidie astrahentem nos gratiam Dei humiliter subsequamur*[27]—daily to follow humbly, to the very last step, the grace of God which draws us in. He specifies a bit more in detail the meaning of the adverb "humbly" by appealing to the repentance of David: *quod peccatum suum humiliatus agnoscit, suum est.*[28] David's part is to recognize his sinfulness and God's part is to pardon him. "After having been humiliated (*humiliatus*)," writes Cassian, which is to say, "humiliated by his weakness" after having passed helter-skelter through the trying fires of temptation—or even, in the case of David, the bitter failure of sin. What is finally important—as one of the sayings already has hinted—is that such an experience is the only way left to God to make us conscious at once of our weakness and God's grace. One of the fathers said, "I prefer a defeat borne humbly than a victory obtained by pride."[29] Saint Bernard says nothing different: "God prefers a repentant sinner to a self-righteous virgin."

The Breaking of the Heart

We are now at the heart of the process where one day humility will be born. Confusion lies here at the center. To describe it, along with the interior upheaval it involves, the old monastic literature borrows from their contemporary versions of the Bible an expression which then still possessed all the vigor and

26. *Century* 2.54; Isaac treats the same theme of weakness and the help of God in *Discourse VIII.*
27. *Conference* XIII.3.
28. *Conference* XIII.13.
29. *Vitae Patrum* XV: 74.

suppleness of the image which inspired it: *diatribe tes kardias* or in Latin: *contritio cordis* or *contritio mentis*. We find this expression in all the languages where we encounter the most ancient testimonies of the monastic experience which proves the extraordinary importance which the ancient monastic writers accorded it. Moreover, in Cassian's writings we frequently find it conjoined to the term "humility" where it is practically a synonym and to which it adds a concrete emphasis: *contritis et humiliatis cordibus*[30]—in humble and contrite hearts. As much as possible it would be useful to preserve the rough and abrupt aspect of the original which has unfortunately lost its true sense in most of our modern languages. It is plainly not a question here of "contrition" such as we meet in current spiritual writing but rather of a heart broken or crushed—literally, reduced to shards.

Among other ancient texts, we recall the moving description of the harassment and temptations recounted in that Egyptian text attributed to Macarius the Great known by its title: "A Letter to His Sons." In that text we find temptation following on temptation, each more humiliating than the last while the monk—teetering each time more closely to a fall—has the impression that he has already given in until grace—a force of the Holy Spirit as Macarius calls it—intervenes in the end to save him. Why so many crises repeated over and over and why so arduous? It is because God wishes to teach him, explains Macarius, "that it is God who gives him strength. The monk now truly understands how to give glory to God in the midst of total humiliation and from the depths of a broken heart as David says: 'the sacrifice God requires is a broken heart' (Ps 50:19). For it is from this difficult combat that humility, that broken heart, goodness and mercy issue forth."[31]

Such a description of a distress approaching despair experienced at the heart of temptation, abounded in the literature of the monastic tradition, and should suffice to rebut definitively the myth of "monk as champion ascetic" which was popularized

---

30. *Conferences* IX:36.1; XII:4:10; XX:6-7. Cassian uses *contritio spiritus* once: *In hac humilitate cordis et spiritus contritione* (XX:7)—in that humility of heart and contrition of spirit.

31. *Lettre a ses Fils* 12 (Editions de Bellefontaine, 1985) 76.

by Romantic historiography of the early 1900s. At the heart of temptation, the monk (indeed, every Christian) is no more than a poor servant of Yahweh reduced to the simple level which is a kind of frantic trust in grace. "Believe me, my brother," says Isaac the Syrian, "you have not yet understood the force of temptation and the subtlety of its artifices." One day, however, experience will teach you and "you will find yourself before temptation like an infant who cannot tell which way to look. All your knowledge will be turned into confusion like that of a little child. Your spirit, now seemingly firmly established in God and your knowledge so precise, and your thoughts so well balanced—all will be submerged into a sea of doubt. One thing alone will then help you in overcoming them: humility. The moment you seize upon humility, the power of all your doubts will suddenly disappear."[32]

To align oneself with this divine demanding pedagogy is, of necessity, to accept a movement in its direction, i.e., not to flee humiliation inflicted by temptation but rather to embrace humiliation in a certain sense but not on account of some dark senseless masochism but because one senses that there is the secret source of the only true life. To put it in scriptural terms: it is because it is there that the heart of stone will be broken and a heart of flesh will be revealed which had been hidden for a time behind so many unconscious defenses. In fact, this rupture constitutes, in the arena of psychology, a formidable test first for the narcissistic mirror which accompanies us everywhere and which literally shatters into pieces. Further, for the pharisee hidden in our heart, we can no longer save face. And even more it is precisely here, as the ancient authors insist, that it is crucial to follow grace down to the last vestige because in the midst of accepting a humiliation—or perhaps better: spiritually "digested"—that salvation awaits us. As an ancient saying advises: "When we are tempted, let us abase ourselves even more, for then God will protect us—He who sees our weakness. But if we elevate ourselves, he removes his protection from us and we perish."[33] Or, as another saying counsels us: "Submit yourselves in the grace of God in a spirit of

---

32. *Discourse* 57.
33. *Vitae Patrum* XV: 67.

poverty (*subditus esto gratiae Dei in spiritu paupertatis*)—lest you be ensnared by a spirit of pride and lose the fruits of your labors."[34]

Such then, according to the Fathers, is the task of the human being in the sad confrontation between, on the one hand, a freedom wounded by sin, and, on the other hand, God's restorative grace which is at one and the same time so subtle and so perfectly sovereign. This task is the requisite passage through humiliation which is the indispensable condition of authentic humility as well as any other virtue which will prove not to be an illusion reflected above all in our narcissistic mirror or flatteringly approved by our virtuous superego. Even chastity is, in this regard a gift from God, in that it is not possible, thinks Cassian, except for those who welcome it into a heart completely broken: "*his . . . solumnodo qui Deo totat spiritus sui contritione deservium.*"[35] The human task, torn between freedom and grace, is the peaceful acceptance of a broken heart. It is a question of the emptiness or a void which is there to welcome nothing more than grace. If there is effort involved, it's that which belongs to human fragility perpetually confronted by its own limits. Cassian hails it—with no little grandeur—as a *perpetua humilitas* or rather a humiliation without end. This takes us into the very heart of the gospel as well as to the nodal point of asceticism and all Christian mysticism. According to Pseudo-Macarius it is the very foundation of the Christian faith: "to have a heart wholly broken."[36]

A Christian Askesis

There are those temptations which God sends to us which are, without a doubt, the best temptations while there are others that we choose for ourselves. As noted earlier, it is perhaps in this sense that the particular path of the monk seems to run ahead of temptation in embracing a way of life in which a freely accepted life of asceticism occupies a relatively important place. Does that make the monk stronger than others? That would be the

---

34. *Vitae Patrum* XV:55; see: *Apothegmata* OR 13. (The Greek text says: "Submit yourself to the grace of Christ.")

35. *Conference* XIII.5.

36. *150 Chapters* 114.

supreme illusion. In fact, the reverse is true. If the monk chooses a life of asceticism—even if he chooses it in some confusion—it is because he must be exposed in his own eyes as the weakest of all. An authentically Christian asceticism has the same status as temptation and necessarily initiates the same process whose end will produce the same fruits of humility and love, *humilis caritas*, humble love. Without this, humility would be a perfectly pagan enterprise in which Aristotle or Cicero might be recognized themselves perhaps but not the Jesus of Easter morning. As Isaac the Syrian reminds us: "So long as someone is not humble, he will receive no recompense for his asceticism. Recompense is not given on account of asceticism, but on account of humility . . . no more is recompense given on account of virtue, but rather for humility, which is born of the two. When humility is lacking, asceticism and virtues are in vain."[37]

Far from being a punishment, temptations and trials comprise the distinctive way in which God arranges for us to be in some measure satisfied some day. In fact, thinks Isaac the Syrian, God continually holds in reserve "diversions and consolations without number" with which he wishes to inundate us, while our lack of aptitude and preparations for them obliges God to send us "affliction in place of diversion, correction in place of aid."[38] Isaac writes about this further: "As soon as grace observes that a little self-satisfaction has slipped into someone's thoughts and that he has begun to have a good opinion of himself, grace permits the temptations on the battlefield to become stronger and even to get the upper hand until such time as the man learns to recognize his weakness and to flee from it in order to hold fast humbly to God. For it is in this way that one acquires through faith in the Son of God, the stature of the perfected human being, and is elevated to love."[39]

It is not only temptation which is the school of humility; it is sin itself which is permitted by God when he seems to have exhausted other means; sin can become a pathway to salvation. It will suffice for us to recall King David, from whom—as said

37. *Discourse* 57.
38. *Discourse* 26 in the Brock edition. CSCO 125 (Leuven, 1975) 125ff.
39. *Discourse* 72.

in Psalm 50—the spiritual tradition has borrowed the image of the "contrite and humiliated heart." David had clearly and truly fallen into sin but it was sin that for him became a *felix culpa* (a happy fault) and which put him on the path to salvation.

In a homily entirely dedicated to humility Saint Basil invokes in this sense the fall of the Apostle Peter. Peter loved Jesus more than any other person but he thought a bit too much of himself. God "delivered him over to his own human cowardice and, as a consequence, he fell into denying Jesus but his fall made him wise and put him on his guard. He learned to spare the weak having experienced his own weakness. He understood clearly that it was through the power of Christ that he had been rescued when he was in danger of perishing from his lack of faith in that tempestuous storm when he had been saved by the right hand of Christ when he was about to sink under the waters."[40] Basil concluded a bit further on, "It is humility which often frees the one who most frequently and gravely sins." That explains why Saint Isaac of Nineveh does not hesitate to call the lapses of a monk the "guardians" of his justification. God permits these lapses, Isaac writes, "so that transgressions and failings become occasions for humility. It is humility that protects the greatest ascetical labors of monks not only to avoid pride but also humiliating them by the recollection of their faults. It is in this fashion that they receive again an even greater recompense."[41] For if they do not experience some temptation even the greatest gifts of God are "a disaster for those who receive them. . . If God supplies you with some gift, beg him that he might teach you how this gift can help you progress in humility . . . or else beg him to remove the gift from you so that it might not become the cause of your downfall. Not everyone has the capacity of being so blessed without causing some kind of damage to themselves."

If from temptation there is a fall it is not because one lacks generosity but rather because humility was lacking. The occasion of sin, if the sinner is alert to the grace which never ceases to work within him, can help him, in the end, to find that narrow and lowly, quite lowly, gate which alone opens out into the King-

---

40. *Homily* XX.4.
41. *Discourse* 57 (Brock edition) 283–285.

dom of God. "It is crucially important not to despair that we are not what we ought to be," advises Saint Peter of Damascus. "O course, your sin is an evil thing but if you say 'there is the place where my condemnation lies but still more is that place where God's mercy lives' then you are repentant and God receives your repentance as he receives the repentance of the prodigal son. . . Whoever sins but does not despair, lowers himself beneath all other creatures. He dares not to condemn or blame any person. Rather, he marvels at the love of God for humanity and gives thanks to his Benefactor. If he does not follow the devil who, under the power of sin, pushes him towards despair, then his lot is cast with God. He possesses within himself the power of grace, patience, and the fear of the Lord . . . he does not judge lest he himself is judged."[42] It is possible that the most perfidious temptation is not the one which precedes sin but rather the one which follows sin: the temptation to despair from which humility—once learned—will allow one to escape.

The sentiment which, in the end, will prevail for the truly humble person is an unshakeable confidence in God's mercy of which he has tasted at least a glimmer even in the midst of failure. How then could he doubt it any longer? It is once again Isaac the Syrian who sketches a portrait for us, one so near to our own daily experiences. In a text from a recently discovered corpus of his writings Isaac asks: "Who, then could be troubled by the memory of his sins? . . . will not God pardon me for those things which grieve me and the memory of which torments me? Those things which, even though they horrify me, I still allow myself to dwell upon again and again? When those sins were committed they caused more suffering than the sting of a scorpion. I abhor them and yet seem to find myself always in their midst; when, full of sorrow, I have repented of them, nevertheless I return to them unfortunate as I am." And those, Isaac adds, "are the thoughts of so many people who fear God, who aspire to virtue, and who regret their sins even while their weakness forces them to take account of the errors that causes them. They constantly live suspended between sin and repentance." However Isaac continues, "Do not doubt your salvation. . . God's mercy extends beyond

42. Book I.

what you can possibly conceive and his grace is much greater than you ever could require. He watches without ceasing for the slightest hint of remorse from the person who permits the smallest impulse of justice to appear in battle with passions and sin."[43]

This divine game between temptation and grace is a game of love. Far from being a taskmaster, God reveals himself in this game as a teacher who is infinitely loving and patient, gentle and humble of heart, who always labors to fashion us in his image. Perhaps it has been Saint John Cassian who has sketched out for us the most touching portrait. Along with the story of our temptations Cassian sees a picture of the unparalleled kind heartedness of God. He goes so far as to compare it to the tender playfulness existing between a mother and child with the goal of easing the child's development into adulthood. "For a long time she carries the baby in her arms," writes Cassian, "until finally she teaches him to walk. First, she lets him crawl about. Then she sits him upright and supports him with her right hand in order that he might learn how to place his feet, one in front of the other. Soon, she lets him go for an instant but the moment she sees him totter she catches him up again and supports his hesitant steps. She picks him up or even holds him back from a fall or perhaps even lets him fall softly so that she might pick him up again. . ." It is in that manner, concludes Cassian, "that the heavenly Father acts towards each of us.[44] He knows best that we 'who must be held upon the lap of his grace (*in sinu gratiae suae*)' must be put to the test under his care. He leaves us master of our own freedom all the while aiding us in our labors, responding to us when we call upon him, refusing to abandon us when we seek him, and sometimes even rescuing us from danger without our knowledge."[45] More than at any other time, it is in the hour of temptation that we find ourselves "in the lap of his grace."

The humility which comes into being at that hour cannot be reduced to the greater or lesser degree of esteem that one holds for oneself. This humility is of an entirely different order for it transcends the realm of qualities and virtues; it must be identified

43. *Discourse* 40 (Brock edition) 178–179.
44. *Conference* XIII.14.
45. *Ibid.*

with a new being born from the grace of baptism and bringing forth all of baptism's fruits. If one still wishes to speak in the language of virtue it would be an all encompassing virtue—the heart of stone shattered and restored to life as the heart of flesh—the virtue from which all other virtues are derived. As Isaac the Syrian describes it: "Humility is the garment of God."[46]

Such a person may consider himself weak and sinful but he ends up turning his eyes away from misery in order to contemplate only the mercy of God. His brokenheartedness and his contrition are unknowingly transformed into a humble and peaceful joy, into love, and the action of grace. No fault or sin is ignored or excused but, rather, they are submerged and engulfed in mercy. Where sin abounds, grace yet more abounds (Rom 5:20). Whatever sin has destroyed is restored; indeed, improved far beyond what it once was—by grace. Our prayer still bears the traces of sin and wretchedness—and without doubt, always will—but henceforth the fault is a happy one, a *felix culpa*, as we sing each Easter vigil for our culpability is swallowed by love. There is, then, almost no discrimination between temptation and the action of grace. They are intertwined and the tears of repentance are also the tears of love.

Little by little this joyful sense of repentance begins to predominate spiritual experience. Out of this discipline of poverty—*patientia pauperum*—a new person arises each day completely and wholly defined by peace, joy, kindness, and gentleness. Such a one is forever marked by penitence but it is a penitential spirit that is full of joy and full of a love which appears plainly visible in him, everywhere and always and which remains as a backdrop for the entire quest for God. Such a person has henceforward attained a profound peace because his whole being has been destroyed and rebuilt by grace. He hardly recognizes himself. He has become a different person. He has nearly touched the abyss of sin but at the same time has plunged into the abyss of God's mercy. He has finally learned to put down his weapons before God and to surrender himself. He has renounced his quest for personal righteousness and abandoned any project of sanctity. His hands are empty—or, perhaps better, hold nothing more than

46. *Discourse 77.*

his own wretchedness—but he dares to expose them to mercy.
God has finally become God for him and nothing but God. He
desires only to say: *Salvator!* Savior from sin. He has even almost
been reconciled with his own sinfulness just as God has been reconciled with him. He is content to recognize his own weakness.
He no longer seeks to perfect himself: "All of us have become
impure/ all our good deeds are like polluted rags" (Is 64:5). His
righteousness rests in God alone. Only his wounds remain to
him but even these have been nursed and healed by mercy and
have burst forth miraculously into health. He knows nothing
any longer except how to give thanks and praise to God who is
always at work in him in order to bring forth marvelous things.

To his brethren and friends, he has become a kind and gentle
friend. He understands their weakness. He no longer has confidence in himself but in God alone. He lives his entire life in the
grip of God's love and power. That is why he is poor—truly poor,
poor in spirit—and is close to all those who are poor and to all
kinds of poverty both spiritual and material. He numbers himself
first among sinners—but a forgiven sinner. That is why he can
walk a path in the world as an equal and a brother of all sinners.
He considers himself close to them for he understands that he
is no better than any of them. His most intimate prayer is that
of the Publican—a prayer which has become for him almost like
breathing, like the heartbeat of his entire being, his deepest desire
for salvation and healing: "Lord, have mercy on me, a sinner."

There, then, remains in his heart only one desire: that God
put him once more to the test so that he might discover more pro-
foundly God's immediacy, so that he might once more embrace
humble patience and unreservedly surrender himself to God
with even greater love. He longs for the suffering and humility
which draws him closer to Jesus and allows God to renew within
him his wonders.

At the beginning of this exposition I wished to summon to
the bar the testimonies of several philosophers, both pagan and
Christian, in order to cast doubt on their ability to understand,
by reason alone, the humility found in the Gospel. I would like to
conclude by using the words of another philosopher, a Christian
one, named Jean Guitton. In his last work, written when he was
nearly one hundred years old and only months from his death,

he gave us what he called his *Philosophical Testament*.[47] In a narrative characterized by elegance as much as by humor, he pictures himself on his deathbed, receiving a final visit with all the great ones with whom he had rubbed shoulders either in the flesh or through ideas while on earth. They paraded before him one after the other "Blaise Pascal, Henri Bergson, Paul VI (who was a great friend), El Greco, Leopold Senghor, General DeGaulle (of whom he was a great admirer), Socrates, Maurice Blondel, Dante, and Francois Mitterand (in whom he had great confidence). All these personalities came to help prepare him for the Judgment he was about to undergo at the moment of his impending death. His case was not to be decided in advance. He was aware of all the barely avoided traps he had encountered in his life dedicated to philosophy not the least of which, he confessed, was his penchant for arrogance and vainglory. However, he was saved at the last, partially through the intercession of Saint Thérèsè of the Child Jesus, and in part on account of the final words given him by the Judge just before deliberations began over his fate. Let us listen to those words which Guitton borrows from one of the greatest mystics of all times. "Jesus then asked me: Jean have you anything at all to add?" I replied, "I stand before you Jesus, my Creator, my Savior, and my Judge." As I spoke these words I attempted to pull out of my pocket a piece of paper which I finally managed to do. I tried to unfold it but, overcome with emotion, the paper fell to the ground. At that moment, Thérèsè leapt forward. . . She picked up the paper. I was extremely tired. In a flat voice I said to Teresa, "read it yourself. It is from Ruusbroec the Admirable. That is how I would have loved to live and die." Thérèsè then read: "When a man considers deeply, with eyes burnt with love, the immensity of God . . . and when that same man takes account of all his outrages against the great and faithful Lord . . . he can think of no contempt great enough to satisfy himself . . . he falls into the grip of a strange bewilderment—he is bewildered by his inability to heap sufficient scorn upon himself . . . he thus surrenders himself to the will of God, and in the most intimate self abnegation finds true peace, a peace that cannot be disturbed by

47. *Testament Philosophique* (Paris: Presses de la Renaissance, 1997). Guitton died in 1999 [trans. note].

anything. Even one's sins become for us a source of humility and love. . . To be plunged into humility is to be plunged into God, for God is the foundation of that abyss. . . Humility obtains for us things which are too lofty to be taught or explained; humility attains and possesses what even speech cannot."

PART II

SOME SELECTED TEXTS
ON HUMILITY

Some New Testament Texts

"Come to me all you that are weary and are carrying heavy burdens and I will give you rest. Take my yoke upon you, and learn from me, for I am gentle and humble in heart and you will find rest for your souls. For my yoke is easy and my burden is light." (Mt 11:28-30)

***

"All who exalt themselves will be humbled, and all who humble themselves will be exalted." (Mt 23:12; see: Lk 14:11; 18:14)

***

"But the tax collector, standing far off, would not even look up to heaven, but he was beating his breast and saying 'God, be merciful to me a sinner.' I tell you, this man went down to his home justified rather than the other; for all who exalt themselves will be humbled, but all who humble themselves will be exalted." (Lk 18:13-14)

***

"I, therefore, a prisoner in the Lord, beg you to lead a life worthy of the calling to which you have been called, with all humility and gentleness, with patience, bearing one another in love, making every effort to maintain the unity of the Spirit in the bond of peace." (Eph 41:3)

***

"Finally, all of you, have unity of spirit, sympathy, love for one another, a tender heart and a humble mind." (I Pet 3:8)

"And all of you must clothe yourselves with humility in your dealings with one another, for

'God opposes the proud
but gives grace to the humble.'" (Proverbs 3:34 LXX)

"Humble yourselves, therefore, under the mighty hand of God so that God may exalt you in due time." (I Pet 5b-6)

"But God gives all the more grace; therefore it says: 'God opposes the proud/but gives grace to the humble.' Submit yourselves therefore to God." (James 4:6-7)

"Let the same mind be in you that was in Christ Jesus,
who, though he was in the form of God,
did not regard equality with God
as something to be exploited,
but emptied himself,
taking the form of a slave,
being born in human likeness.
And being found in human form,
He humbled himself
and became obedient to the point of death—
even death on a cross . . . ." (Phil 2:5-8)

"But our citizenship is in heaven and it is from there that we are expecting a savior, the Lord Jesus Christ. He will transform the body of our humiliation so that it may be conformed to the body of his glory." (Phil 3:20-21)

The Monks of the Egyptian Desert (3rd and 4th Centuries)

Abba John the Dwarf said: "Humility is the gate to God and our fathers who have passed through innumerable humiliations enter the City of God with joy." Again he said: "Humility and fear of God surpass all other virtues."

"As breath comes from the nostrils so does a person need humility and fear of God." [Abba Poemen]

"As long as we are in the monastery, prefer obedience to asceticism. The former teaches pride; the latter, humility." [Amma Syncletica]

A brother asked Abba Poemen: "How ought we to act in the place where we dwell?" "Show discretion towards a stranger; show respect to the Elders; do not impose your own point of view; then, you will live in peace."

Archbishop Theophilus of Alexandria went one day to Scete. The brethren gathered together and Abba Pambo said to them: "Give our Father a word of edification." One of the Elders said: "If my silence does not edify, my words would be worth even less."

One day some old men came to see Abba Anthony and Abba Joseph was with them. Wishing to test them the old man suggested a text from the Scriptures and beginning with the youngest asked them what the text meant. Each gave an answer as he was able to do so. Last of all he asked Abba Joseph: "How would you explain this saying?" and he replied, "I do not know." Then Abba Anthony said: "Indeed, Abba Joseph has found the way for he has said, 'I do not know.'"

There was an Elder who had fasted for seventy weeks eating only once during a week. He begged God to elucidate the sense of a passage of scripture but God did not help him. He said to himself, "Well, I have made so much effort to no purpose so I will go to the brethren to get the text clarified." Just as he was closing the door to go out an angel was sent to him by the Lord saying: "For seventy weeks you fasted without complaint to God; You are humble enough to ask your brothers the true sense of the text so I have been sent by God to reveal the real sense of the text." After the clear sense of the text had been explained to him, the angel left him.

Humility is the ground upon which the Lord commands us to offer our sacrifice.

A brother once asked an Elder: "Give me a word which I can hold in my heart and live with." The Elder responded: "If you are insulted and can take it, you possess a great thing which undergirds all virtue."

Abba Anthony said to Abba Poemen: "Here is the great task for a man: to accept in himself his sin before God and expect temptation until he takes his last breath."

Again, Abba Anthony said: "Anyone who has not been tempted cannot enter the Kingdom of Heaven." He further added: "Without temptation, one cannot be saved."

Abba Anthony said: "I saw all the snares of the Enemy spread out over the world and groaned saying 'What can get through such traps?' I heard a voice saying to me, 'Humility.'"

One day Abba Arsenius was being terribly assaulted by demons who had come to torment him. Some disciples came to visit him and while still outside his cell heard him cry out to God: "Lord, do not abandon me. I have never done anything good in your presence but in your infinite goodness, grant me to begin to do so."

An Elder said: "If anyone says 'pardon me' in genuine humility, it burns all the demonic tempters."

John the Dwarf said: "We have put aside a light burden which is self-accusation only to take up the heavy one which is self-justification."

Someone asked an Elder what humility was. He responded: "Humility is a great and divine thing. The road of humility is made from the fatigue of the body and the rejection of sin and of other things also." A brother said to him: "What does the 'good of other things' mean?" The Elder replied: "Never to see the sins of others but always to see one's own sins and beg God for forgiveness incessantly."

An Elder was asked: "What do you make of those who claim 'we have visions of angels?'" He responded: "Blessed are those who never lose sight of the vision of their own sins."

Before Abba Poemen and his followers came to Egypt there was an Elder in Egypt who had fame and a wide reputation. When Abba Peomen came to Scetis some left the Elder to go up and see Abba Poemen. Abba Poemen was upset by this saying to his disciples: "What can we do for this Elder who is hurt that some left him to visit us who are nothing? What can we do to console the Elder?" He then said: "Prepare a little food and get a skin of wine and we will go and visit him to eat with him. In that way, we can comfort him." So they put together the repast and took off. When they knocked at the Elder's door one of his disciples asked who they were. They answered: "Tell the abba that it is Poemen who desires a blessing from him." The disciple reported this but the old man said to tell them to go away for he had no time for them. Despite the heat, they insisted saying: "We shall not go away until we have met the Elder." Seeing their humility and their patience the Elder was stung with compunction and opened his door to them. They went in and ate. During the meal the Elder said: "Truly, not only what I have heard about you is true but I see that it is a hundred times more true." When they parted on that day he became their friend.

Abba John the Dwarf asked: "Who sold Joseph?" A brother replied: "His brothers." The Abba replied: "No, it was his humility which sold him because he could have said 'I am their brother' in objection but because he kept silent he sold himself by his humility. It is also his humility that made him the chief in Egypt."

Abba Isaiah said: "To love human glory is the result of untruth but to resist it with humility increases the fear of God in one's heart. Do not become ever a friend of the great of this world so that the fear of God weaken in you."

An Elder said: "If one gives an order to a brother in humility and the fear of God it will incline the brother to submit and do what is demanded of him. If, on the other hand, giving orders to a brother without fear of God and in a spirit of domination with an idea of exerting authority, God, who knows the secrets of the heart, will not inspire that brother to hear and submit. In fact, that which is done according to God is easily recognizable just as is an order done in an authoritarian way and through one's own will. That which is asked according to God is asked in humility and through prayer; that which is ordered with a spirit of domination reflects anger and disturbance coming from the Evil One."

Aphrahat the Persian Sage (3rd and 4th Centuries)

Humility is the testimony of the goods which come from the fear of God.

If you look for merciful love you will find it among the humble ones: humility is the place where justice resides.

Instruction belongs to the humble ones; from their lips comes understanding.

Humility brings forth wisdom and discernment; humble people possess prudence.

If you are looking for chastity and patience you will find it among the humble ones.

The word of a humble person is sweet and his face radiant; he blossoms and is joyous.

Love shines forth among the humble; the wise understand that it is to them that they should go for guidance.

The humble resist all malevolence and on their face shines the goodness of their heart.

The humble person speaks as he should but with a smile on his lips, never raising his voice.

A humble person has a horror of arguments since they produce jealousies.

To ward off words of anger the humble person shuts up his ears so that no such words can reach his heart.

The thinking of a humble person produces a bounty of good thoughts and his spirit meditates on that which is beautiful.

A humble person takes in good teachings like water; they are like oil which penetrates into the fibers of his being.

The eyes of the humble look at the earth but the eyes of their heart are on the supreme things above.

Humility is the fountainhead of peace and the streams of peacefulness flow from it.

Basil of Caesarea (330–379)

[Selections from a Homily on Humility]

Tell me why you should be proud? "What do you possess that you have not received? But if you have received it, why are you boasting as if you have not received it?" (I Cor 4:7). You have not known God by reason of your justice but God has given it to you out of His goodness. "You know God or, rather, to be known by God" (Gal 4:9). You did not attain God by your own power but Christ apprehended you by his coming. "I continue my pursuit in hope that I may possess it since I have been taken possession of by Christ" (Phil 3:12). The Lord tells us: "You have not chosen me but I have chosen you" (Jn 15:16).

Yet you desire to glorify yourself for having received such honors and are proud of the mercy shown you? Know yourself for what you are: Adam expelled from paradise; Saul abandoned by the spirit of God; Israel cut off at its holy roots. "You are there because of faith. Do not become proud but stand in awe!" (Rom 11:20). Judgment will be accompanied by grace.

If you do not understand that you have received grace and by an excess of stupidity ascribe to yourself the success which is a gift of grace, you are no better than Saint Peter. In fact, you will not be able to surpass Peter's love who loved him so ardently that he desired to die for him. Yet, through his boasting, he spoke, saying: "Though all may have their faith in you shaken, mine will never be" (Mt 26:33), but God left him to his folly and he fell a victim to cowardice. He learned from his own weakness to be forgiving to the weak; he came to understand that truth just as when he was lifted up by the helping hand of Christ when he was sinking in the sea.

Christ had seen all this when he said "Simon, Simon behold Satan has demanded to sift all of you like wheat but I have prayed that your own faith may not fail and once you have turned back, you must strengthen all your brothers" (Lk 22:31). Peter, thus reproved, obtained the aid of Our Lord. He gained the strength to renounce his own pride in order to give aid to those who were weak.

Imitate the Lord who descended from heaven to utter abasement and who was, in turn, raised to the glory that was reserved for Him. In everything the Lord did we see the foundation of humility. As an infant he was laid in a manger and not on a bed. In the house of a carpenter and his poor mother he was raised. He made himself subject to his mother and her husband. He was taught and listened to what was needed though he had no need to be told. He asked questions and in his questions showed wisdom.

The Lord submitted himself to John, his servant, in his baptism. He did not resist his enemies with his tremendous power but, yielded to all, even though he had power. He allowed himself to be brought before the chief priests; he allowed himself to be brought before the governor and submitted to his judgment and though he could have refuted his accusers he suffered in silence their calumnies. He was spat upon by slaves and menial servants and condemned to death—a death which according to the judgment of men, was a most infamous death.

From his birth to his death he suffered affliction and after having suffered all those humiliations he showed forth his glory to those who had been his companions, who themselves underwent ignominy and dishonor.

Among those first followers were his disciples who, poor and destitute, went throughout the world, without the power of earthly wisdom and fine speech, as wanderers and solitaries, traveling on land and sea, scourged, stoned, hunted and finally, killed.

These are the divine teachings given to us by our fathers. Imitate them so that from our own humility may we rise up to eternal glory which is the true and perfect gift of Christ our Lord.

Evagrius of Pontus (399)

Just as gold ore when fired in the crucible becomes more and more pure, so the monk who begins on the road of perfection, finds his actions shine little by little in the life of the community, and sparkle in accord with his capacity for perseverance. In fact, by submission to the commands of his brethren, he slowly learns obedience and through reproaches he is disposed more to patience. Every time he accuses himself of offenses with joy and embraces humility with simplicity, he begins to overcomes the passions with which he is at war. He thus may continue his struggle with virtue giving him always more power by grace.

Just as one goes down into the bowels of the earth to find gold, so the one who humbles himself with the gold of humility extracts all virtues. [*To Eulogios*]

"When he is dealing with the arrogant, he is stern, but to the humble he shows kindness" (Pr 3:34).

The Lord resists injustice because he is Justice and the liars because he is the Truth. He likewise resists the proud because he is Humility itself. [*Scholion on Proverbs 3:34*]

Pseudo Macarius (4th–5th Centuries)

If one sees a person puffed up by arrogance and pride because he has received grace and even if he should perform signs and should raise up the dead, if he, nevertheless, does not hold his soul as abject and humble and does not consider himself poor in spirit and an object of abhorrence, he is duped by the devil and is ignorant. Granted he has performed signs but he is not to be trusted. For the sign of the Christian is this, that one is pleasing to God so as to seek to hide oneself from human eyes. And even if a person should possess the complete treasures of the king, he should hide them and say repeatedly: "The treasure is not mine but another has given it to me as a charge. I am a beggar and when it so pleases, he can claim it from me." If anyone should say "I am rich. I have enough. I possess goods. There is nothing more I need." Such a person is not a Christian but a vessel of deceit and of the devil, for the enjoyment of God is insatiable and the more one tastes and eats the more one hungers. Persons like this have an ardor and love towards God that nothing can restrain. And the more they apply themselves to the art of growing in perfection, the more they count themselves as poor, as those in great need, and possessing nothing. This why they say "I am not worthy that the sun shines its rays on me." This is the sign of the Christian, namely, this very humility. [*Spiritual Homily 15.37*]

John Cassian (4th–5th Centuries)

A humility of heart must be maintained which is genuine and which does not come from an affected humbleness of body and speech but from a deep humbleness of mind. It will glow with the clearest indication of patience precisely when a person does not boast to others about crimes of his that are not to be believed, but rather disregards what is insolently said against him by someone else and endures insults inflicted upon him with a gentle and placid heart . . .

True patience and humility are not acquired or held onto without profound humility of heart. If they proceed from this source they will stand in need of neither the benefit of a cell nor the refuge of solitude. For whatever is sustained from within by the virtue of humility, which is the begetter and guardian, does not require the protection of anything.

Iperechios (5th Century)

Humility makes the tree of life grow to its highest.

Note how your failures and your humility are goods: they lead to heaven.

O monk; here is the reward of humility: The Kingdom of Heaven. Don't be deprived of it.

Equality among all the brothers drives out pride and gives root to humility.

A monk who speaks kindly and with humility brings forth tears from a heart of stone.

Abba Isaiah (AD 491)

Above all things, my beloved brothers, cultivate humility. Accept rebuffs and everything that causes suffering. Be on guard always to resist your own will which is the loss of all virtues. For those who cultivate their thoughts with rectitude shall receive grace and sweetness and will fear discord the way one fears a dragon. It is a fact that discord topples the entire spiritual edifice and darkens the mind to the point that one cannot distinguish the light of virtue.

Pay attention to this terrible passion which changes virtue into disorder. . . If a person in effect does not resist this passion he cannot progress on the road to God; all matters of evil fall in place bringing forth impatience and vainglory. In a violent and proud soul one finds everything displeasing to God and the one who pretends to be of God, is, as scripture insists, a mockery.

To pray to God is purity of heart.
If you do not over estimate yourself you will receive the gift
of tears.
Not to judge is true love.
Not to judge your neighbor is greatness of heart.
A heart that loves God does not answer evil with evil.
True recollection consists of not bringing attention to one's
self.
To accept one's own faults brings peace.
Accepting everything brings peace.
To give alms is, above all, to grant pardon.

All of the above cultivates the renunciation of one's own will. Such an attitude grants peace and virtues and places the mind in an atmosphere of quiet.

In all of scripture, in the final analysis, the one thing God asks of a person is to be humble in all things with respect to the brethren, to renounce one's own will, to turn to God at every moment asking God to come to one's assistance, and to shield one's eyes from the sleep of forgetfulness and the trickery of enslavement.

Barsanuphius of Gaza (5th and 6th Centuries)

Answer of Barsanuphius to a brother who decided to give no orders to anyone but to follow a simple rule to take care only of his own self.

Brother, you know that one who will not accept sufferings will not come to glory and those who do not accept gall will not taste sweetness. You have been placed in the midst of brothers and of affairs and for these affairs to be purified are purified by the fire for it is by fire alone that gold is purified. Do not impose anything on yourself absolutely for you are committed to combat and its cares; it is better to judge your opportunities out of fear of God and never for personal reasons. Do all that you can while avoiding anger and become a model for all, neither judging or condemning people, but deal with all as true brothers. Love those who put you to the test, just as I have loved those who put me to the test. In fact, if we reflect well, such persons help us in our own progress. Don't impose a rule; be obedient and humble and render each day an account of yourself. The prophet underscores that "each day" when he says "I will call to mind the deeds of the Lord. . ." (Ps 77:11) and Moses: "And now, O Israel. . ." (Dt 4:1). Pay attention to that "now." And if you must give orders to someone examine your own thinking; if it never seems worth the trouble or seems useful, hold your tongue and think of what He once said "What does it benefit a man to gain the whole world and lose his own soul?" (Mt 16:26). Look, my brother, every thought in which calm and humility does not reign, does not come from God; by contrast, every thought coming from the enemy comes with anger and trouble. Certain thoughts seem to come dressed in the fleece of a lamb but underneath those skins are rapacious wolves. One can recognize the troubles which they can provoke for it is written "By their fruits you shall know them" (Mt 7:16). God is with us and understands all and will not allow us to be bound up by injustice for in God's eyes "all is naked and laid bare" (Heb 4:13). You, my beloved brother, take on all that is demanded of you, keeping before your eyes the fear of God always giving Him thanks. For, from God comes all grace, strength, and power through all the centuries. Amen!

Dorotheus of Gaza (5th–6th Centuries)

An Elder said: "Above everything, you must have humility and be able to say 'pardon' for every word is addressed to you because humility every evil deed of the Adversary. . . No virtue is attainable without humility. . . Humility is truly great. Every saint has walked this road of humility and, thanks to their efforts, they have a shortened road as it is written: 'consider all my afflictions and my trouble and forgive all my sins' (Ps 25:18). In fact, it is through humility alone that one is able to gain entrance to the Kingdom of heaven . . ."

I recall that one day we were speaking about humility. A dignitary from Gaza listening to us speak about these matters saw himself as a sinner and was puzzled. "How is all this possible?" he asked. He refused to listen to what was said resisting every explanation. "My dear sir," I said to him, "what do you consider yourself to be in your town?"

A great dignitary—the first citizen of my town.
If you were to go to Caesarea how would you be considered?
Inferior to those of that city.
And if you were to go to Antioch?
I would be considered a village rustic.
And at Constantinople in the court of the emperor?
As a miserable bumpkin.

"Well then," I said to him, "the saints are like that. When they draw near to God they sense themselves to be as the greatest sinners."

All the saints that we know of have acquired humility by observing the commandments. Nobody learns about it from words nor is it an inborn quality if it is not learned from experience. Nobody learns humility from sermons.

One day Abba Zosima was speaking of humility. A teacher of rhetoric who happened to be there wished to know the precise meaning of his words and asked him: "Tell me how it is possible that you consider yourself a sinner? Don't you realize that you are a saint adorned with virtues? Look how you obey the commandments! How do you dare call yourself a sinner?" The elder did not know how to answer but was compelled to answer "I don't know the answer but it is true." However, the teacher kept insisting. Seeing that the elder could not explain himself I said to him: "Is it not the same thing with the art of rhetoric or the practice of medicine? When one begins to learn about an art, little by little, by the very practice of the art, one gains the mentality of the rhetor or the doctor but it is very difficult to say how the skill was acquired. Little by little, as I have said, one acquires expertise. It is the same thing with humility; obedience to the commandments brings forth a profound disposition towards humility which cannot be explained in words . . ."

A brother asked an elder: "What is humility?" The elder answered: "Humility is a great and divine exercise. The path of humility is made of physical labors accompanied by discernment, by regarding one's self as lower than everyone and to pray unceasingly. That is the path of humility but humility itself is divine and is beyond all understanding."

Saint Benedict of Nursia (5th–6th Century)

Brothers, divine scripture calls to us saying, "Whoever exalts himself shall be humbled, and whoever humbles himself shall be exalted" (Lk 14:11; 18:14). In saying this, therefore, it shows us that every exaltation is a kind of pride, which the prophet indicates he has shunned, saying, "O Lord, my heart is not exalted; my eyes are lifted up and I have not walked in the ways of the great nor gone after marvels beyond me" (Ps 130[131]:1). And why? "If I had not a humble spirit, but were exalted instead, then you would treat me like a weaned child on my mother's lap" (Ps. 130[131]:2).

Accordingly, brothers, if we want to reach the highest summit of humility, if we desire to attain speedily that exaltation in heaven to which we climb by the humility of this present life, when by our ascending actions we must set up that ladder on which Jacob in a dream saw "angels descending and ascending" (Gen 28:12). Without doubt, this descent and ascent can signal only that we descend by exaltation and ascend by humility. Now the ladder erected is our life on earth, and if we humble our heart the Lord will raise it to heaven. We may call our body and soul the sides of the ladder, into which our divine vocation has fitted the various steps of humility and discipline as we ascend.

The first step of humility, then, is that a man keep the "fear of God" always "before his eyes" (Ps 35[36]:2) and never forget it. He must constantly remember everything God has commanded, keeping in mind that all who despise God will burn in hell for their sins, and all who fear God have everlasting life awaiting for them. While he guards himself at every moment from sins and vices of thought or tongue, of hand or foot, of self will or bodily desire, let him recall that he is always seen by God in heaven, that his actions everywhere are in God's sight and are reported by angels at every hour.

The prophet indicates this to us when he shows that our thoughts are always present to God, saying, "God searches hearts and minds" (Ps 7:10) and again he says "The Lord knows the thoughts of men" (Ps 93[94]:11) and likewise "From afar you know my thoughts" (Ps 138[139]:3) and "The thoughts of men shall give you praise" (Ps 75[76]:11). That he may take care to avoid sinful thoughts, the virtuous brother must always say to himself: "I shall be blameless in his sight if I guard myself from my own wickedness" (Ps 17[18]:24).

Truly, we are forbidden to do our own will, for scripture tells us "Turn away from your desires" (Sir 18:30). And in the Prayer too we ask God that his "will be done" in us (Mt 6:10). We are rightly taught not to do our own will since we dread what scripture says "There are ways which men call right that in the end plunge us into the depths of hell" (Prov 16:25). Moreover, we fear what is said of those who ignore this: "They are corrupt and have become depraved in their desires" (Ps 13[14]:1).

As for the desires of the body, we must believe that God is always with us, for "all my desires are known to you" (Ps 37[38]:10) as the prophet tells the Lord. We must then be on guard against any base desire, because his death is stationed near the gateway of pleasure. For this reason scripture warns us "Pursue not your lusts" (Sir 18:30).

Accordingly, if "the eyes of the Lord are watching the good and the wicked" (Prov 15:3), if, at all times, "the Lord looks down from heaven on the sons of men to whether any understand and seek God" (Ps 13[14]:2); and if every day the angels assigned to us report our deeds to the Lord day and night, then, brothers, we must be vigilant every hour or, as the prophet says in the psalm, God may observe us "falling" at some time into evil and "so made worthless" (Ps 13[14]:3). After sparing us for a while because he is a loving Father who waits for us to improve he may well tell us later, "This you did and I said nothing" (Ps 49[50]:21).

The second step of humility is that a man loves not his own will nor takes pleasure in the satisfaction of his desires; rather he shall imitate by his actions that saying of the Lord "I have come not to do my will, but the will of him who sent me (Jn

6:38). Similarly, we read: "Consent merits punishment; constraint wins a crown."

The third step of humility is that a man submits to his superior in all obedience for the love of God, imitating the Lord of whom the apostle says "He became obedient even unto death" (Phil 2:8).

The fourth step of humility is that in this obedience under difficult, unfavorable, or even unjust conditions, his heart quietly embraces suffering and endures it without weakening or seeking escape. For scripture has it: "Anyone who perseveres to the end will be saved" (Mt 10:22) and, again, "Be brave of heart and rely on the Lord" (Ps 26[27]:14). Another passage shows how the faithful must endure everything, even contradiction, for the Lord's sake, saying in the person of those who suffer, "For your sake we are put to death continually; we are regarded as sheep marked for slaughter" (Rom 8:36; Ps 43[44]:22). They are so confident in their expectation of reward from God that they continue joyfully and say "But in all this we overcome because of him who so greatly loved us" (Rom 8:37). Elsewhere scripture says "O God, you have tested us, you have tried us as silver is tried by fire; you have led us into a snare, you have placed afflictions on our backs" (Ps 65[66]:10-11). Then, to show that we ought to be under a superior, it adds: "You have placed men over our heads" (Ps 65[66]:12).

In truth, those who are patient amid hardships and unjust treatments are fulfilling the Lord's command: "When struck on one cheek, turn the other; when deprived of their coat, they offer their cloak also; when pressed into service for one mile, they go two (Mt 5:39-41). With the apostle Paul they bear "with false brothers, endure persecution, and bless those who curse them" (2 Cor 11:26; 1 Cor 4:12).

The fifth step of humility is that a man does not conceal from his abbot any sinful thoughts entering his heart or any wrongs committed in secret but rather confesses them humbly. Concerning this, scripture exhorts us "Make known your way to the Lord and hope in him" (Ps 36[37]:5). And again: "Confess to the Lord, for he is good; his mercy is forever" (Ps 105[106]:5). So too the prophet: "To you I have acknowledged my offense; my faults I have not concealed. I have said: against myself I will report my faults to the Lord and you have forgiven the wickedness of my heart" (Ps 31[32]:5).

The sixth step of humility is that a monk is content with the lowest and most menial treatment and regards himself as a poor and worthless workman in whatever task he is given saying to himself with the prophet: "I am insignificant and ignorant, no better than a beast before you, yet I am with you always" (Ps 72[73]:22-23).

The seventh step of humility is that a man not only admits with his tongue but is also convinced in his heart that he is inferior to all and of less value, humbling himself and saying with the prophet, "I am truly a worm and no man, scorned by men and despised by the people" (Ps 21[22]:7). And "I was exalted when I was humbled and overwhelmed with confusion" (Ps 87[88]:16) and again "It is a blessing that you have humbled me so that I can learn your commandments" (Ps 118[119]:71, 73).

The eighth step of humility is that a monk does only what is endorsed by the common rule of the monastery and the example set by his superiors.

The ninth step of humility is that a monk controls his tongue and remains silent, not speaking unless asked a question, for scripture warns: "In a flood of words you will not avoid sinning" (Pr 10:19) and a "talkative man goes about aimlessly on earth" (Ps 138[14]:12).

The tenth step of humility is that he is not given to ready laughter, for it is written "Only a fool raises his voice in laughter" (Sir 21:23).

The eleventh step of humility is that a monk speaks gently and without laughter, seriously, and with becoming modesty, briefly and reasonably but without raising his voice, as it is written: "A wise man is known by his few words."

The twelfth step of humility is that a monk always manifests humility in his bearing no less than in his heart so it is evident at the Work of God, in the oratory, the monastery or the garden, on a journey or in the field or anywhere else. Whether he sits, walks, or stands, his head must be bowed and his eyes cast down. Judging himself always guilty on account of his sins, he should consider that he is already at the fearful judgment and constantly say in his heart what the publican in the Gospel said with downcast eyes: "Lord, I am a sinner, not worthy, to look up to heaven" (Lk

18:13) and with the prophet: I am bowed down and humbled in every way" (Ps 37[38]:7-9; 118[119]:107).

Now, therefore, after ascending all these steps of humility, the monk will quickly arrive at that "perfect love" of God which "casts out fear" (I Jn 4:18). Through this love, all that he once performed with dread, he will now begin to observe without effort, as though naturally, from habit, no longer out of fear of hell but out of love for Christ, good habit and delight in virtue. All this the Lord will by the Holy Spirit, graciously manifest in his workman now cleansed of vices and sins.

John Climacus (6th–7th Century)

Real repentance, mourning scrubbed of all impurity, and holy humility among beginners are as different and distinct from one another as yeast and flour from bread. The soul is ground and refined by visible repentance. The water of true mourning brings it to a certain unity. I would even go so far as to speak of a mingling with God. Then, kindled by the fire of the Lord, blessed humility is made into bread and made firm without the leaven of pride . . .

The first and principal result of this excellent and admirable triad is the sweet readiness of the soul to accept indignity, to receive it with open arms, to welcome it as something that relieves and cauterizes diseases of the soul and grievous sins. The second result is the erasure of anger—and modesty over the fact that it has subsided. Third and preeminent is the honest distrust of one's own virtues, together with a desire to learn more . . .

The monk who has humility as his bride will be gentle, inclined towards compunction, sympathetic, peaceful in every situation, radiant, easy to get along with, inoffensive, alert and active. In a word: free from passion. "The Lord remembered us in our humility and delivered us from our enemies" (Ps 135[136]:23-24).

Let not your soul be a hollow in the stream of life, a hollow sometimes full and sometimes dried up by the heat of vainglory and pride. Instead, may your soul be a spring of dispassion that wells up into a river of poverty. . . The valley is a soul made humble among the mountains of work and virtues. It always remains free of pride and steadfast. In scripture are the words "I humbled myself and the Lord hastened to rescue me" (Ps 115[116]:6). And these words are there instead of "I have fasted" or "I have kept vigils" or "I lay down upon the bare earth."

Repentance lifts a man up. Mourning knocks at heaven's gate. Holy humility opens it up. This I say and I worship a Trinity in Unity and a Unity in Trinity.

The sun lights up everything visible. Humility reaches across everything done according to reason. Where there is no light, all is in darkness. Where there is no humility, everything is in decay.

There is a difference between contrition, self-knowledge, and humility.

Contrition is the outcome of a lapse. One who has lapsed breaks down and prays without arrogance, though with laudable persistence, disarrayed and yet clinging to the staff of hope; indeed, using it to drive off the dog of despair.

Self-knowledge is a clear notion of one's own spiritual advance. It is also an unwavering remembrance of one's slightest sins.

Humility is a spiritual teaching of Christ led spiritually like a bride into the inner chamber of the soul deemed worthy of it, and it somehow eludes all description.

Humility is like a heavenly waterspout which can lift a person from the abyss of sin to heaven's height.

Someone discovered in his heart how beautiful humility is and, in his amazement, he asked her to reveal her parent's name. Humility smiled, joyous and serene: "Why do you rush to learn the name of my begetter? He has no name, nor will I reveal him to you until you have God for your possession. To whom be glory forever!" Amen.

The sea is the source of the fountain and humility is the source of discernment. [*The Ladder of Divine Ascent—chapter 25*]

Isaac the Syrian (7th Century)

Knowledge of God and knowledge of self gives birth to humility. [*Arabic Maxim #24*]

Humility of heart is born in a person from two sources: full awareness of one's sins and contemplation on the humility of Our Lord.

A humble person does not upset anyone. He is not upset by anyone. He remains unnoticed; he remains unknown like the soul which is unseen and unknown. The humble person is the soul and consolation of the world.

My brothers, whenever the moment comes to speak to you of the heavenly source of humility I am filled with fear just as anyone would be who tries to use his own words to speak of God. In point of fact, humility is the clothing of God through the Word who was made flesh; He has taken on our humanity to speak to us through our own fleshliness. Whoever takes on the clothing of humility becomes like that One who came down from on High to mask his glory so that the whole of creation would not have perished at the sight of Him. Creation in fact could not have seen Him except in the manner which he appeared and through which he spoke. Creation heard his words from his mouth but it wished to see God. Without that [mask] the children of Israel could not have heard his voice except that he spoke out of a cloud.

Those who don the cloak of humility by changing his body in holiness, like the Creator who revealed himself and as Christ himself did through his incarnation, will reveal himself to all of the world.

If God allows one to experience great misery it can make him to become weak hearted. One becomes low spirited along with a sense of suffocation in the soul; an experience like a taste of hell. At such times of this spirit of confusion a person feels paralyzed and subject to numerous temptations: turbulence, anger, abuse, dishonor, a vacillating will, a need to move about constantly from one place to another and other such maladies. If you were to ask me what causes all of this I would answer: yourself because you lack the means to uproot such evils. There is a remedy for all of these temptations by means of which someone can obtain peace of soul. And what is that remedy? Humility of heart! Without humility, in point of fact, a person beats at the walls that make up such evils but finds them impregnable. If you resist hearing this truth you will never search the depths of your soul. If you do search you will find that these evils will disappear one after the other.

You can bear all your problems to the degree that you are humble. Your capacity to bear your difficulties will be lightened and you will find consolation for your soul; the depth of that consolation will increase your love for God; and the depth of that consolation will grant you joy in the Spirit . . .

When one understands the need of God's help, he is driven to prayer and the force of that prayer makes for humility of heart. Anyone, in fact, who does not feel this need and does not ask for help, is not humble.

The one who knows the self knows all things. To search the self deeply is to see the fullness of all things. Just as everything is in the self, the knowledge of the self embraces the knowledge of everything and in the submission of the self is to submit to all things.

When humility fills one's whole life you will submit yourself to all because within your heart the peace of God issues forth. In consequence of that, you will instantly find not only the vanquishing of the passions but also of everything that happens to you.

In truth, O Lord, if we do not know how to humble ourselves you will never cease to humble us. True humility is the child of knowledge and true knowledge is the child of temptations . . .

Anyone who is truly humble need never seek out humility since it will be in him almost naturally and will come to a humble person without labor. That person will receive it within himself like a grace that goes beyond creation and nature and will think of himself in his own estimation as a sinner and as one who is contemptuous. That person will live within all spiritual realities; he will possess the wisdom of all creation but he will know with certainty that he is nothing. In his heart he is humble without doing anything about it or in any way forcing himself.

But is it really possible that such a person becomes such that his very nature has been transformed in such a way? There can be no doubt about it for this mysterious power which he has received brings to perfection every virtue. It is the mysterious power itself which the apostles received under the form of tongues of fire which is to say the Paraclete, the Consoler Spirit. As it was said in scripture "He leads the humble in what is right; and teaches the humble his way" (Ps 25:9). That text shows that the humble ones are able to receive in themselves that Spirit of revelation which uncovers mysteries.

However, one might ask: How to do this? How does one gain such humility? By what means am I worthy to receive such a gift? I chastise myself and when I think that I have acquired humility I soon learn that impulses contrary to it afflict my spirit and I fall into despondency.

To anyone who poses such questions Scripture answers: "It is enough for the disciple to be like the teacher and the slave like the master" (Mt 10:25). The one who demands humility of us will grant the grace to acquire it. Imitate Our Lord and you will find it. Those who have imitated these things and sanctified their lives also give glory to Him who comes from the Father and who sent the Spirit now and always and forever and ever. Amen. [*Selection from Ascetic Discourse*]

John Bar Kaldun (10th–11th Century)

Authentic humility, beloved brothers, is worthy of all praise which we have already showered on Rabbi Yusef Busnaya and it is worthwhile repeating him once again: It is from God that humans receive form from dust and is made similar to God. And, further, God has pity on all things and loves everything and that is exactly how a humble person must act.

Saint Bernard of Clairvaux (1090–1153)

The prophet said "I myself was humbled greatly" (Ps 115:10). In my own eyes I fell very low.

The psalmist has been humbled and now stands on the first step of truth. As he says in another psalm "In your truth you have humbled me" (Ps 118:75). Up to this point he has been examining himself. Now he looks out from himself, to others and passes to the second step of truth, exclaiming in his excess "Every man is a liar." What is meant by "in his excess"? It means that he was carried away by feelings and compassion. What did he mean? He meant that every man is unreliable because too weak, helpless, and infirm to save himself or others. It is in the same sense that the Psalmist says that "the horse is a deceptive hope of safety (Ps 32:17). The horse does not deceive anyone but a man deceives himself when he trusts too much in the horse's strength. That is what is meant by saying that "every man is a liar." He is fragile and fickle and hope in him is deceptive either for himself or for others. Indeed, there is a "curse on the man who puts his hope in man" (Jer 17:5). So the humble Prophet is led along his way by truth. He is grieved at what he found in himself. He now sees the like in others. Sorrow and truth mount up together in him (see Eccles 1:18) and he bursts out into the sweeping but true statement "Every man is a liar". . .

. . . When in the light of truth men know themselves and so think less of themselves it will certainly follow that what they loved before will now become bitter for them. They are brought face to face with themselves and blush at what they see. Their present state is no pleasure to them. They aspire to something better and at the same time realize how little they can rely on themselves to achieve it. It hurts them and they find some relief in judging themselves severely. Love of truth makes them hunger and thirst after justice (see Mt 5:6) and conceive a deep contempt for themselves. They are anxious to exact from themselves full satisfaction and real amendment. They admit that to make satisfaction is beyond their powers—when they have done all that is commanded they acknowledge that they are still unprofitable servants (see Lk 17:10). They fly from justice to mercy, by the road that Truth leads them: "Blessed are the merciful for they shall obtain mercy" (Mt 5:7). They look beyond their own needs to the needs of their neighbors and from the things they themselves have suffered they learn compassion; they have come to the second degree of truth.

If they persevere in these things: sorrow of repentance, desire for justice, and works of mercy they will cleanse their hearts from the three impediments of ignorance, weakness, and jealousy and will come through contemplation to the third degree of truth . . .

It occurs to me that it is possible to allot each of these three works to one of the Persons of the Undivided Trinity, that is, in so far as a man still sitting in darkness (see Lk 1:79) can make distinctions in the work of the Three Persons who always work as one. There would seem to be something characteristic of the Son in the first stage, of the Holy Spirit in the second, and of the Father in the third. What is the work of the Son? "If I your Lord and Master have washed your feet, how much more ought you also to wash another's feet?" (Jn 13:14). The Master of truth gave his disciples an example of humility and opened to them the first stage of truth. Then the work of the Holy Spirit: "Charity is spread abroad in our hearts by the Holy Spirit who is given to us" (Rom 5:5). Charity is a gift of the Holy Spirit. By it those who, under the instruction of the Son were led to the first step of truth by, humility now under the guidance of the Holy Spirit reach compassion for their neighbor. Finally, listen to what is said of the Father: "Blessed are you Simon, son of John, for flesh and blood have not revealed it to you but my Father who is in heaven" (Mt 16:17). Again: "The Father will make known the truth to the sons" (Is 38:19) and "I will confess to you, Father, for you have hidden these things from the wise and made them known to the little ones" (Mt 11:25). You see: by word and example the Son first teaches men humility; then the Spirit pours out his charity upon whom the Father receives finally into glory.

. . . if he [Christ] submitted himself to human misery so he might not simply know of it, but experience it as well, how much more ought you not make any change in your condition, but pay full attention to what you are, because you are truly full of misery. This is the only way, if you are to learn to be merciful. If you have eyes for the shortcomings of your neighbor and not for your own, no feeling of mercy will arise in you but rather indignation. You will be more ready to judge than to help, to crush in the spirit of anger than to instruct in the spirit of gentleness. "You who are spiritual, instruct such a one in the spirit of gentleness" says the Apostle (Gal 6:1). His counsel, or better, his precept is that you should treat an ailing brother with the spirit of gentleness with which you would like to be treated in your own weakness. He shows them how to find out the right way to apply this spirit of gentleness: "Considering yourself lest you also be tempted" (Gal 6:1).

It is worth noticing how closely the Disciple of Truth follows the order of his Master's thoughts. In the beatitudes, just as the merciful as I have said, come before the clean of heart, so the meek are spoken of before the merciful. When the Apostle tells the spiritually minded to instruct the earthly minded he adds: "In the spirit of meekness" (Gal 6:1). In other words, one cannot be merciful if he is not humble. Thus the Apostle clearly shows what I promised to prove to you, namely, that we must look for truth first in ourselves and afterwards, in our neighbor. "Considering yourself," he says, that is, considering how easily you are tempted and how prone to sin, you will become meek and ready to help others in the "spirit of gentleness." If the words of the Disciple do not impress you enough perhaps you will take warning from the stern words of the Master: "Hypocrite, first cast the beam from your own eye and then you will see better to cast the mote from your brother's" (Mt 7:5). The heavy thick beam in the eye is pride of heart. It is big, but not strong, swollen, not solid. It blinds the eye of the mind and blots out the truth. While it is there you cannot see yourself as you really are, or even the ideal of what you could be but what you would like to be, this you think you are or hope to be. For what else is pride but, as a saint [i.e., Saint Augustine] has defined it, the love of one's excellence. Neither love nor hate will give an impartial judgment. Truth will judge thus: "As I hear, so will I judge" (Jn 5:30). Not: "as I hate" nor "as I love" nor "as I fear." Hate gave his judgment: "We have a law and according to the law he ought to die" (Jn 19:7). Fear spoke: "If we let him alone, the Romans will come and take away our place and our nation" (Jn 11:48). And we have an example of judgment swayed by love when David said of his parricide son: "Spare the boy Absalom" (Sam 18:5). I understand that it is the practice of both ecclesiastical and civil courts, in accord with the law, to forbid special friends of litigants to try their cases lest love of their friends blind the judges or tempt them to act unfairly. If love can make you blind or too lenient in regard to the faults of a friend, what will your self love do when you consider your own faults? [*The Steps of Humility and Pride*—passim]

SELECT BIBLIOGRAPHY

Alfeyev, Hilarion. *The Spiritual World of Isaac the Syrian* (Kalamazoo, MI: Cistercian, 2000).

Brock, Sebastian. *The Syriac Fathers on Prayer and Humility* (Kalamazoo, MI: Cistercian, 1987).

————. *The Wisdom of Saint Isaac of Nineveh* (Oxford: SLG, 1997).

Chryssavgis/Penkett, trans. *Abba Isaiah of Scetis: Ascetic Discourses* (Kalamazoo, MI: Cistercian, 2002).

Conway, Ambrose. *Bernard of Clairvaux: The Steps of Humility and Pride* (Kalamazoo, MI: Cistercian Publications, 1989).

Driscoll, Jeremy, trans. *Evagrius of Pontus: Ad Monachos* (New York: Newman/Paulist, 2003).

Fry, Timothy, ed. *The Rule of St. Benedict in Latin and English* (Collegeville, MN: Liturgical Press, 1981).

Funk, Mary Margaret. *Humility Matters* (New York: Continuum, 2005).

Gregg, Robert, trans. *Athanasius: The Life of Antony* (New York: Paulist, 1980).

Harmless, William. *Desert Christians: An Introduction to the Literature of Early Monasticism* (London and New York: Oxford University Press, 2004).

Louf, André. *Teach Us to Pray* (London: Darton, Longman and Todd, 1979).

————. *The Cistercian Way* (Kalamazoo, MI: Cistercian, 1983).

————. *Turning into Grace* (Kalamazoo, MI: Cistercian, 1992).

————. *Mercy in Weakness* (Kalamazoo, MI: Cistercian, 1998).

————. *Humility* (London: Catholic Truth Society, 2005).

Luibheid, Colm, trans. *John Climacus: The Ladder of Divine Ascent* (New York: Paulist, 1982).

Maloney, George A., trans. *Pseudo Macarius: The Fifty Spiritual Homilies and the Great Letter* (New York: Paulist, 1992).

Meyer, Robert, trans. *The Lausiac History* (New York: Newman/Paulist, 1965).

Palmer/Sherrard/Ware, trans. *The Philokalia: The Complete Text* 3 volumes (London and Boston: Faber & Faber, 1979).

Price, R. M., trans. *A History of the Monks of Syria by Theodoret of Cyrrhus* (Kalamazoo, MI: Cistercian, 1985).

————. *Lives of the Monks of Palestine by Cyril of Scythopolis* (Kalamazoo, MI: Cistercian, 1991).

Ramsey, Boniface, trans. *John Cassian: The Conferences* (New York: Paulist, 1997).

————. *John Cassian: The Institutes* (New York: Newman/Paulist, 2000).

Rousseau, Philip. *Basil of Caesarea* (Berkeley, CA: University of California Press, 1994).

Russell, Norman, trans. *The Lives of the Desert Fathers* (Kalamazoo, MI: Cistercian, 1981).

Spidlik, Tomas. *The Spirituality of the Christian East* (Kalamazoo, MI: Cistercian, 1986).

————. *Prayer: The Spirituality of the Christian East* (Kalamazoo, MI: Cistercian, 2005).

Stewart, Columba. *Cassian the Monk* (New York: Oxford University Press, 1998).

Vivian/Athanassakis, trans. *The Life of Antony: The Coptic and the Greek Life* (Kalamazoo, MI: Cistercian, 2003).

Ward, Benedicta, trans. *The Sayings of the Desert Fathers: The Alphabetical Collection* (Kalamazoo, MI: Cistercian, 1984).

————. *The Sayings of the Desert Fathers (The Anonymous Series)* (Oxford: SLG Press, 1986).

Wheeler, Eric, trans. *Dorotheos of Gaza: Discourses and Sayings* (Kalamazoo, MI: Cistercian, 1977).